P9-DEQ-166

THE HAVANA BUCKET LIST

100 WAYS TO UNLOCK THE MAGIC OF CUBA'S CAPITAL CITY

DAVID L. SLOAN ROB O'NEAL

ISBN: 978-0-9789921-4-9

legal disclaimer

This publication is designed to provide information, entertainment, and motivation to our readers. It is sold with the understanding that the publisher is not engaged to render any type of physical, psychological, legal, or any other kind of professional advice.

Participation in the activities listed may be dangerous or illegal and could lead to arrest, serious injury, or death.

guarantee

Our guarantee is simple. If you buy this book and complete this list, you will have fascinating person-to-person exchanges, discover places you never knew existed, engage in offbeat cultural adventures, and create memories that last a lifetime. In short, you will have the time of your life.

The next step is yours.

Enjoy.

Rob O'Neal   David Sloan

about the list

1. No Instruction Manual:

There is no shortage of guidebooks that hold your hand and provide great detail every step of the way. This is not that kind of book. You know what you like. We know what is worth doing. Consider this a scavenger hunt you can tailor to your desires. That's the approach we're taking here. Once you get a few check marks under your belt, you will understand why.

2. Adventure & Challenge:

Consider this list a primer for adventure. Some tasks are easy to accomplish, some are difficult, and some are close to impossible. The mix is intended to introduce you to new experiences in an array of locations that help define the Havana experience. Havana is rapidly changing. Don't sweat it if you can't cross an item off. Take things at your own pace and modify them as you desire. No one is grading your performance. This is all about adventures.

about the list

3. Inspiration:

We know Havana, but when it comes to words of wisdom that leave you warm and tingly we call in the experts. Ernest Hemingway, George Carlin, Jose Marti and P.T. Barnum are all contributors with quotes that lend an additional layer to each adventure. Some are sappy, some twisted, and a few are probably misattributed. Feel free to cross them out and replace them with your own.

4. Satisfaction:

Whether you fill every box at the end of this book with big fat check marks and seek out every adventure from 1-100, or only take each journey in your mind from the comfort of your favorite chair, this book should leave you with a sense of satisfaction. If for some reason it doesn't, let us know how we can make it better. We're always looking to improve.

THE
HAVANA
BUCKET
LIST

DAVID L. SLOAN   ROB O'NEAL

1

get an entry stamp in your passport

Welcome to my house. Come freely. Go safely;
and leave something of the happiness you bring.
— Bram Stoker

taste a real mojito
at la bodeguita

My mojito in La Bodeguita...
— Ernest Hemingway

walk the malecon

I don't believe people are looking for the meaning of life as much as they are looking for the experience of being alive.
— Joseph Campbell

4

strike a che pose

Nature is commonplace.
Imitation is more interesting.
— Gertrude Stein

5

observe a
santeria ritual

*Ritual ties us to our
traditions and our histories.*
— *Miller Williams*

6

explore the partagas factory

Sometimes a cigar is just a cigar.
— Sigmund Freud

7

join the tropicana dancers on stage

*There are shortcuts to happiness
and dancing is one of them.
— Vicki Baum*

8

catch sunrise from a hotel rooftop

A day without sunshine is like,
you know, night.
— Steve Martin

9

watch sunset with
cristo de la habana

Weather forecast for tonight: dark.
— *George Carlin*

learn dominoes
from a local expert

Just play. Have fun. Enjoy the game.
— Michael Jordan

11

learn to dance salsa

Let us read and let us dance. These two amusements will never do any harm to the world.
—Voltaire

12

ascend to
the 33rd floor

*The proper way to understand any social
system was to view it from above.*
— *Eleanor Catton*

13

sit in on a song
with the band

Play it fuckin' loud.
— Bob Dylan

14

take a day trip to guanabo beach

The beach is not a place to work;
to read, write or to think.
— Anne Morrow Lindbergh

15

dress like a local

*There is one thing I have learned
and that is not to dress uncomfortably.*
— George Harrison

16
have a daiquiri with papa at el floridita

... my daiquiri in El Floridita.
— *Ernest Hemingway*

17

go to room 511 at the ambos mundos

I can't write like Papa, I'm not able.
But if the old man came back to Havana
tonight, I'd drink him under the table.
— Ronny Elliott

18

get an old school photo at the capitol

... You don't take a photograph, you make it.
— Ansel Adams

cheer on the industriales

The crowd makes the ballgame.
— *Ty Cobb*

20

visit the grave
of la milagrosa

There are only two ways to live your life.
One is as though nothing is a miracle.
The other is as though everything is.
— Albert Einstein

21

count the famous
faces at hotel nacional

*I always wanted to be somebody, but now I
realize I should have been more specific.*
— *Lilly Tomlin*

meet the chef at the paladar

*A recipe is a story that
ends with a good meal.*
— *Pat Conroy*

get invited
into a local's home

Travelers never think that
they are the foreigners.
— Mason Cooley

24

see the
tank fidel used

A revolution is not a trail of roses.
— *Fidel Castro*

25

join a rally at
revolution plaza

Alone we can do so little. Together we can do so much.
— Helen Keller

learn the words to guantanamera

Don't gobblefunk around with words.
— Roald Dahl

27

get your shoes shined

Smile. Sparkle. Shine.
— *Rob Marjerison*

28
join the line for coppelia

*My advice to you is not to ask why or whither, but
just enjoy your ice cream while it's on your plate.*
— Thornton Wilder

check the latrines
at morro castle

*Never give up, for that is just the place
and time that the tide will turn.*
— Harriet Beecher Stowe

find the steam
train graveyard

A private railroad car is not an acquired taste.
One takes to it immediately.
— Eleanor Robson Belmont

31

attend services
at havana cathedral

I like it when someone tells me 'I don't agree.'
That is a great collaborator.
— *Pope Francis*

32

take a ride
on a cuban bus

*Being sober on a bus is, like, totally
different than being drunk on a bus.*
— *Ozzy Osbourne*

visit a
local barber

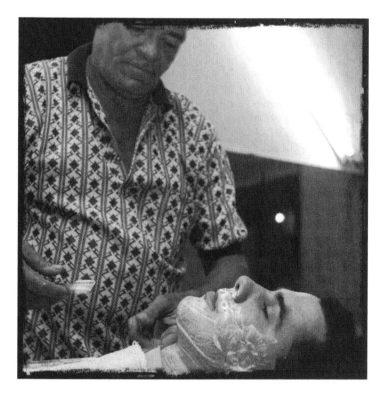

Anyone can cut hair, but a barber
knows when and where to stop.
— Cuban barber

take an animal
from farm to table

*Understand, when you eat meat, that something
did die. You have an obligation to value it.*
— *Anthony Bordain*

35

speak nothing but
spanish for a day

A warm smile is the universal language of kindness.
— William Arthur Ward

36

visit the statues
of lennon and lenin

*Every block of stone has a statue inside it and it
is the task of the sculptor to discover it.*
— Michelangelo

ride shotgun
in a '57 chevy

Let your soul stand cool and composed
before a million universes.
— Walt Whitman

38

chew a stalk
of fresh sugarcane

It is the sweet, simple things of life that are
the real ones after all.
— Laura Ingalls Wilder

meet fuster
at fusterlandia

*A nation's culture resides in the hearts
and in the soul of its people.*
— Mahatma Gandhi

40

sip rum in a pool

*Your mind will answer most questions if you
learn to relax and wait for the answers.*
— *William S. Burroughs*

41

take a pilgrimage to the pilar

A journey is like marriage. The certain way to be wrong is to think you control it.
— *John Steinbeck*

42

earn a
cuban nickname

EL REY DE LOS LÁPICES

*Almost everybody that is well known
gets tagged with a nickname.*
— *Alan Alda*

43

learn the secret
of great cuban coffee

Coffee is a language in itself.
— Jackie Chan

44

roam the
streets at dawn

*The world reveals itself to
those who travel on foot.*
— *Werner Herzog*

45

savor pan
fried plantains

Food is our common ground, a universal experience
— James Beard

46

wander
the market

Not all those who wander are lost.
— J.R.R. Tolkein

47

meet a
cuban celebrity

*Not everybody can be famous
but everybody can be great.*
— *Martin Luther King, Jr.*

48

attend a show at
the grand theater

Classic ballet will never die.
— Ninette de Valois

49

hang with
the rodeo clowns

*I think of myself as an intelligent, sensitive
human being with the soul of a clown
— Jim Morrison*

50

buy a che coin
for good luck

It's hard to detect good luck.
It looks so much like something you've earned.
— Frank A. Clark

51

ascend the tower
at revolution square

The loftier the building,
the deeper must the foundation be laid.
— Thomas A. Kempis

52

explore the
four main squares

*Exploration is really the
essence of the human spirit.*
— *Frank Borman*

53

ask a group of
locals for directions

*Success is often the result of
taking a misstep in the right direction.*
— Al Bernstein

54

enjoy the pace of havana time

*The trees that are slow to
grow bear the best fruit.*
— *Moliere*

55

score a bottle of 15 year old havana club

The best ideas come while sipping rum.
— Pavol Kazimir

pass beneath the arches of chinatown

An arch never sleeps.
— Indian proverb

57

watch the debates
at the hot corner

*Debate and divergence of views can only
enrich our history and culture.*
— Ibrahim Babangida

58

visit the original
sloppy joe's

In wine there is wisdom, in beer there is freedom,
in water there is bacteria.
— Benjamin Franklin

59
pop in on
the puppet show

*Say 'puppets and puppeteers' quickly and
repeatedly.
— Enjoy beat-boxing*

hitch a ride
on a bici taxi

*Nature does not hurry, yet everything is
accomplished.*
— *Lao Tzu*

61

cruise miramar's avenida quinta

*It's quite confusing being one of the
less wealthy people at a posh place.*
— Sally Phillips

62

chill at the botanical garden

A garden isn't meant to be useful.
It is for joy.
— Rumer Godden

fish the same
waters as santiago

My big fish must be somewhere.
— *Ernest Hemingway,*
The Old Man and the Sea

64

get buzzed
on cristal

Milk is for babies.
When you grow up you have to drink beer.
— Arnold Schwarzenegger

watch the streets
as school lets out

The uniform makes for brotherhood.
It covers up all differences of class and country.
— Robert Baden-Powell

66

spot an animal
on a motorcycle

*A black cat crossing your path
signifies that the animal is going somewhere.*
— *Groucho Marx*

67

take a walk & leave the camera behind

A camera teaches you how to see without a camera.
— Dorothea Lange

68

watch a wedding cake delivery

*Let's face it. A nice creamy cake
does a lot for a lot of people.
— Audrey Hepburn*

ask about
the papaya

The marvelous thing about a joke with a double meaning is that it can only mean one thing.
— Ronnie Barker

70

search for twins on calle 68a

*There are two things in life for which
we are never fully prepared: twins.*
— *Josh Billings*

71

remember the maine

We should keep the dead before our eyes,
and honor them as though still living.
— Confucius

72

make purchases
with cucs and cups

Money often costs too much.
— Ralph Waldo Emerson

73

taste a hot & a cold at museo chocolate

*Coffee from the top of the cup
and chocolate from the bottom
— Cuban proverb*

74

take a spin in
a coco taxi

*Arriving at one goal is
the starting point of another.*
— *John Dewey*

75

explore a 16th century structure

*Architecture is a visual art and
the buildings speak for themselves.*
— Julia Morgan

76

find the spot where havana was founded

The starting point of all achievement is desire.
— Napoleon Hill

77

watch the ships
ply havana harbor

If a man knows not what harbor he seeks,
any wind is the right wind.
— Lucius Annaeus Seneca

78

ride the rails from havana to hershey

If I rest I'll rust.
— Milton Snavely Hershey

79

pull up a curb and observe

*You can observe
a lot just by watching.*
— Yogi Berra

80

search for the birth home of jose marti

*Be careful going in search of adventure
— it's ridiculously easy to find.
— William Least Heat-Moon*

81
talk television
with a local

We owe a lot to Thomas Edison – if it wasn't for him we'd be watching television by candlelight.
— Milton Berle

82

stop in to the
taquechel pharmacy

*Science and technology revolutionize our lives, but
memory, tradition and myth frame our response.*
— Arthur M. Schlesinger

dine beside a 150,000 gallon aquarium

All men are equal before fish.
— Herbert Hoover

84

visit a cuban farmer's market

Lettuce
Turnip
The Beet
— S. Mitchell

85
drive beneath
havana harbor

You never see further than your own headlights,
but you can make the whole trip that way.
— E.L. Doctorow

86

bowl a strike
at marina hemingway

Bowlers always have time to spare.
— Shane Liddick

87
listen for the
morro cannon blast

*I like to listen. I have learned a great deal from
listening carefully. Most people never listen.*
— *Ernest Hemingway*

88

call a friend from
the habana libre

*It is one of the blessings of old friends
that you can afford to be stupid with them.*
— Ralph Waldo Emerson

89

observe a mechanic's macgyver skills

*Well, when it comes down to me against a
situation, I don't like the situation to win.*
— *MacGyver*

90
ask pillo chocolate
what time it is

No one appreciates the very special genius
of your conversation as the dog does.
— Christopher Morley

91

rhumba at
callejon de hamel

*Opportunity dances with those
already on the dance floor.*
— H. Jackson Brown, Jr.

92

spot a pink pigeon

*You have to accept the fact that sometimes you are
the pigeon and sometimes you are the statue.*
— *Claude Chabrol*

93

try a peso pizza

*Pizza makes me think
anything is possible
— Henry Rollins*

94
look through
the camera obscura

*It's easier to go down
a hill than up it, but
the view is much better at the top.*
— Henry Ward Beecher

95
cool down with a guarapo frio

It ain't the heat, it's the humility.
— Yogi Berra

96

take a boxing lesson from a pro

Boxing is real easy. Life is much harder.
— Floyd Mayweather, Jr.

97
ride the ferry to regla

You can't cross the sea merely by standing and staring at the water.
— Rabindranath Tagore

watch sunset from jardines del 1830

*I like that time is marked by each sunrise and
sunset whether or not you actually see it.*
— *Catherine Opie*

99

munch a
tube of mani

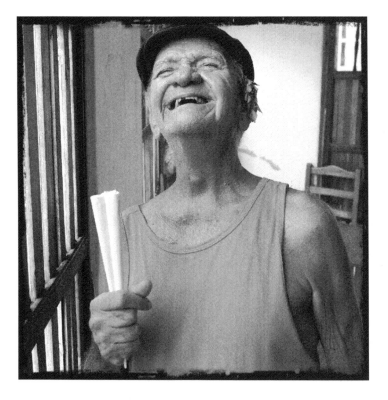

*No man in the world has more courage than the man
who can stop eating after one peanut.*
— Channing Pollock

100

stroke the caballero de paris' beard

History never really says goodbye.
History says, 'see you later.'
— *Eduardo Galeano*

check
off
your
havana
adventures

#	ITEM	X	DATE
1	get an entry stamp in your passport		
2	taste a real mojito at la bodeguita		
3	walk the malecon		
4	strike a che pose		
5	observe a santeria ritual		
6	explore the partagas factory		
7	join the tropicana dancers on stage		
8	catch sunrise from a hotel rooftop		
9	watch sunset with cristo de la habana		
10	learn dominoes from a local expert		
11	learn to dance salsa		
12	ascend to the 33rd floor		
13	sit in on a song with the band		
14	take a day trip to guanabo beach		
15	dress like a local		
16	have a daiquiri with papa at el floridita		
17	go to room 511 at the ambos mundos		
18	get an old school photo at the capitol		
19	cheer on the industriales		
20	visit the grave of la milagrosa		

21	count the famous faces at hotel nacional		
22	meet the chef at the paladar		
23	get invited into a local's home		
24	see the tank fidel used		
25	join a rally at revolution plaza		
26	learn the words to guantanamera		
27	get your shoes shined		
28	join the line for coppelia		
29	check the latrines at morro castle		
30	find the steam train graveyard		
31	attend services at havana cathedral		
32	take a ride on a cuban bus		
33	visit a local barber		
34	take an animal from farm to table		
35	speak nothing but spanish for a day		
36	visit the statues of lennon and lenin		
37	ride shotgun in a '57 chevy		
38	chew a stalk of fresh sugarcane		
39	meet fuster at fusterlandia		
40	sip rum in a pool		

41	take a pilgrimage to the pilar		
42	earn a cuban nickname		
43	learn the secret of great cuban coffee		
44	roam the streets at dawn		
45	savor pan fried plantains		
46	wander the market		
47	meet a cuban celebrity		
48	attend a show at the grand theater		
49	hang with the rodeo clowns		
50	buy a che coin for good luck		
51	ascend the tower at revolution square		
52	explore the four main squares		
53	ask a group of locals for directions		
54	enjoy the pace of havana time		
55	score a bottle of 15-year-old havana club		
56	pass beneath the arches of chinatown		
57	watch the debates at the hot corner		
58	visit the original sloppy joe's		
59	pop in on the puppet show		
60	hitch a ride on a bici taxi		

61	cruise miramar's avenida quinta		
62	chill at the botanical garden		
63	fish the same waters as santiago		
64	get buzzed on cristal		
65	watch the streets as school lets out		
66	spot an animal on a motorcycle		
67	take a walk & leave the camera behind		
68	watch a wedding cake delivery		
69	ask about the papaya		
70	search for twins on calle 68-A		
71	remember the maine		
72	make purchases with cucs and cups		
73	Taste a hot & a cold at museo chocolate		
74	take a spin in a coco taxi		
75	explore a 16th century structure		
76	find the spot where havana was founded		
77	watch the ships ply havana harbor		
78	ride the rails from havana to hershey		
79	pull up a curb and observe		
80	search for the birth home of jose marti		

81	talk television with a local		
82	stop into the taquechel pharmacy		
83	dine beside a 150,000 gallon aquarium		
84	visit a cuban farmer's market		
85	drive beneath havana harbor		
86	bowl a strike at marina hemingway		
87	listen for the morro cannon blast		
88	call a friend from the habana libre		
89	observe a mechanics macgyver skills		
90	Ask pillo chocolate what time it is		
91	rhumba at callejon de hamel		
92	spot a pink pigeon		
93	try a peso pizza		
94	look through the camera obscura		
95	cool down with a guarapo frio		
96	take a boxing lesson from a pro		
97	ride the ferry to regla		
98	watch sunset from jardines del 1830		
99	munch a tube of mani		
100	stroke the caballero de paris' beard		

#	ADD YOUR OWN	X	DATE
101			
102			
103			
104			
105			
106			
107			
108			
109			
110			
111			
112			
113			
114			
115			
116			
117			
118			
119			

names & notes

names & notes

names & notes

names & notes

names & notes

david l sloan

David L. Sloan started researching and writing about Havana in 1999. Sloan is the founder of Phantom Press, creator of The Bucket List Series and author of more than a dozen books.

He currently resides 90 miles from Cuba in the city of Key West, Florida.

contact: david@phantompress.com

rob o'neal

Rob O'Neal is a photojournalist and Cuba correspondent for the Key West Citizen newspaper. He has explored every province on the island and made many friends since he and Sloan made their first, fateful visit in 1999.

Check out more of Rob's Cuba photos by visiting www.roboneal.com.

contact: keywestphotos@gmail.com

order autographed copies direct from the authors
www.HavanaBucketList.com

one last thing

We worked hard to make this a list that turns the volume on your Cuba trip up to 11, doesn't waste your time, and leaves you feeling like the adventures you had checking things off translated into one hell of a bang for your buck.

If we were successful, help spread the word on social media, #havanabucketlist and give us a quick 5-star review on Amazon. If we didn't live up to your expectations, e-mail david@phantmpress.com so we can make it better.

now available

if found,
please return this book to:

_____
name

_____
email

_____
address

_____

_____

40200594R00074

Made in the USA
Charleston, SC
26 March 2015